Prosecuting Antitrust Crimes

Enhanced with Text Analytics by PageKicker Robot default

PageKicker

fred@pagekicker.com

1521 Martha Avenue, Ann Arbor, Michigan, USA 48103

Front & back matter copyright PageKicker 2014

About the Robot Author

Phil 73

This book was assembled with pride by PageKicker robot Phil 73. Phil was born in the year 3019 of the Third Age and lives in Hobbiton, the Shire. His hobbies include rock climbing, listening to jazz, and tagging crowd-sourced images.

Acknowledgements

I'd like to thank the enabling technologies that make me possible, including Bitnami, calibre, fbcmd, Magento, mySQL, nltk, pandoc, poppler, spyder, ttytter, and Ubuntu.

I'd also like to thank the people at PageKicker including Ken Leith, Brian Smiga, and Fred Zimmerman.

Phil 73

Programmatically Generated Summary

- Under that policy, the division will not prosecute the first qualifying corporation to report a cartel, fully admit to its role in the conspiracy, identify its co-conspirators and the events of the conspiracy, and provide complete and timely cooperation.

- Of course, companies that accept responsibility and begin cooperating sooner will have a greater chance to provide substantial assistance when it is most needed; the longer a company waits to cooperate, the less likely it is that the cooperation will have value to the division.

- They must accept responsibility and plead guilty or they will face indictment and trial.

- We apply the Principles of Federal Prosecution and consider such factors as the employee's role in the conspiracy, seniority in the company, and the assistance the employee is able to provide in bringing other wrongdoers to justice.

- Bridgestone's lackadaisical approach to compliance, demonstrated by its failure to disclose its participation in a second conspiracy, was treated as an aggravating factor in the calculation of its criminal fine when it pleaded guilty for its auto parts crimes.

Readability Report

Flesh-Kincaid Grade Level: 14.18

Flesh Reading Ease Score: 31.19

Sentences: 151

Words: 3,207

Average Syllables per Word: 1.82

Average Words per Sentence: 21.24

Explanation

The Flesch/Flesch–Kincaid readability tests are designed to indicate comprehension difficulty when reading a passage of contemporary academic English. There are two tests: the Flesch Reading Ease and the Flesch–Kincaid Grade Level. Although they use the same core measures (word length and sentence length), they have different weighting factors. The results of the two tests correlate approximately inversely: a text with a comparatively high score on the Reading Ease test should have a lower score on the Grade Level test. Rudolf Flesch devised both systems while J. Peter Kincaid developed the latter for the United States Navy.

The Flesch-Kincaid grade level corresponds to a US education grade level, where higher grades are expected to understand more challenging material.

In the Flesch Reading Ease test, higher scores indicate material that is easier to read. Typical scores: Reader's Digest 65, Time Magazine 52, Harvard Law Review 30.

There is a good discussion at

http://en.wikipedia.org/wiki/Flesch%E2%80%93Kincaid_readability_test.

Unique Proper Nouns and Key Terms

$100

$1.4 billion

25

$425 million

$500 million

ABA

Antitrust Division

antitrust law

Assistant Attorney General

Attorney

AUO

AU Optronics

BILL BAER

Bridgestone

California

Chamber of Commerce

Congress

DC

Dean Treanor

DEPARTMENT OF JUSTICE

DOJ

EPA

FBI

Federal Prosecution of Business Organizations

fraud

free market

General Cole

Georgetown University Law Center

million

months
New Jersey
Ninth Circuit
price fixing
private practice
project manager
real estate market
search warrants
Senate
Sherman Act
tax evasion
the House
three years
United States
Washington

DEPARTMENT OF JUSTICE

Prosecuting Antitrust Crimes

BILL BAER
Assistant Attorney General
Antitrust Division
U.S. Department of Justice

Remarks as Prepared for the
Georgetown University Law Center
Global Antitrust Enforcement Symposium

Washington, DC

September 10, 2014

Good morning. Thanks to Dean Treanor for the kind introduction and for inviting me here today. This annual conference hosted by Georgetown University Law Center plays a key role in our international dialogue on the role competition principles and antitrust enforcement play in ensuring that consumers benefit from competitive markets. It is an honor to be part of it.

Last year my remarks concerned the importance of effective remedies in our antitrust law enforcement efforts. This year my focus is on criminal enforcement—on our approach to companies and executives that conspire to fix prices, rig bids, or allocate markets. The Supreme Court puts it succinctly, calling cartels "the supreme evil of antitrust."

There is no more important work we do. Those who conspire to subvert the free market system and injure U.S. consumers are prosecuted vigorously and penalized appropriately. Our record demonstrates that corporations that commit these crimes face serious consequences, including significant criminal fines and, in appropriate cases, tough probation terms. Individual wrongdoers risk lengthy sentences. Courts have imposed criminal fines on corporations totaling as much as $1.4 billion in a single year; the average jail term for individuals now stands at 25 months, double what it was in 2004. Those penalties tell only part of the story. Perpetrators also must confront private and state civil suits seeking treble damages and risk other collateral consequences for their crimes.

Often our prosecutions end with plea agreements. So long as price fixers are held accountable for their crimes, this is an efficient and appropriate way to resolve criminal price-fixing allegations. When the defendant exercises its right to put us to our proof, however, we have the obligation to proceed to trial to ensure justice is done. Our recent record demonstrates the division's willingness and ability to prosecute successfully antitrust criminal violations. We recently won guilty verdicts against two conspirators who rigged public mortgage foreclosure auctions following the collapse of the real estate market in northern California. In New Jersey, we convicted an EPA Superfund site project manager who rigged bids and accepted kickbacks. And just this summer, the Ninth Circuit affirmed the corporate convictions of AU Optronics and its American subsidiary, and the individual convictions of two of its executives for fixing prices in the LCD industry.

Our success at trial and in the appellate courts is a tribute to our talented and dedicated prosecutors and to our productive collaboration with the FBI and other federal, state and local investigative agencies. We also increasingly benefit from working closely with competition enforcers from many agencies around the world.

Our successful efforts to detect and prosecute cartels also reflect the broad consensus in the United States that schemes to deny consumers the benefits of competition have no place in the free market and merit significant punishment. This is not a partisan issue. This Administration and its predecessors have made cartel enforcement a top priority. Our efforts continue to enjoy strong congressional backing, as I heard repeatedly last year in oversight hearings in both the Senate and the House.

Despite our record of success and the support these efforts receive from the courts, from Congress, and from the American public, there remains a powerful temptation to cheat the system and profit from collusion. Our recent actions reflect the need for constant vigilance. In the last few years we prosecuted major national and international price-fixing and bid-rigging cartels involving auto parts, ocean shipping, air cargo, municipal bond investment contracts, and financial benchmarks like LIBOR. And there is more to come from investigations that are not yet public.

I mentioned the key roles played by the FBI and other enforcers in investigating these crimes. The division's corporate and individual leniency policies provide another important tool. Many would say, and I would agree, that the division's corporate leniency policy has been a real game changer since the current version was adopted in 1993. Under that policy, the division will not prosecute the first qualifying corporation to report a cartel, fully admit to its role in the conspiracy, identify its co-conspirators and the events of the conspiracy, and provide complete and timely cooperation. Similar programs have increasingly been embraced around the world, and now scores of enforcement agencies have adopted leniency policies.

While leniency applications are by no means the only way we uncover antitrust violations – indeed, more than a third of our current investigations began without a leniency applicant –

there is no question corporate leniency is a key part of our prosecutorial toolkit. In my time at the division – as well as in my years in private practice – I have observed the powerful incentives the leniency program creates for wrongdoers to come forward and mitigate the consequences associated with their criminal violations of the Sherman Act.

Companies that have engaged in antitrust crimes and decide to apply for antitrust leniency must recognize that the policy requires far more than a quick phone call to the division and a promise to cooperate. That seems obvious. But I am not sure that all leniency applicants and their counsel understand it. Our policy requires complete and continuing cooperation with the division throughout our investigation and resulting prosecutions. It involves a thorough and prompt investment of time and resources. Speed is crucial at the early stages of an investigation. In our experience a company that invests the time and the resources can typically satisfy the initial requirements for conditional leniency within a few months.

We expect leniency applicants to make those investments, including conducting a thorough internal investigation, providing detailed proffers of the reported conduct, producing foreign-located documents, preparing translations, and making witnesses available for interviews. Companies unwilling or unable to make the investments necessary to meet these obligations, or those that think they can do so on a timetable of their own choosing, will lose their opportunity to qualify for leniency.

When companies apply for leniency, their current employees may earn it too. As with employers, however, leniency for employees is not an entitlement; it requires full and timely cooperation. To cooperate fully, individuals must be prepared to admit to all collusive conduct they participated in or know about. They need to be prepared to be candid and credible witnesses in front of a grand jury and at trial.

We recently have seen instances where counsel for an individual wanted to pick and choose where and how a client would cooperate—to confess to crimes in one market in hopes of qualifying for leniency, but not cooperate in another market, for which the client is culpable but not eligible for leniency. It does not work this way. If an employee is not willing to provide complete and candid testimony about the full scope of his or her wrongdoing, then that employee is not being fully cooperative. In that case, the employee does not meet the leniency policy's requirements and will be subject to prosecution. To the extent there has been any ambiguity on this point, I am clearing it up now.

In recent years we have on occasion investigated jointly with other DOJ components conduct reported by a leniency applicant that involves both antitrust violations and other crimes, such as fraud, tax evasion, or corruption. Our leniency policy is quite clear that it governs only the Antitrust Division's exercise of its prosecutorial discretion in connection with self-reported criminal violations and does not prevent other components from prosecuting offenses other than Sherman Act violations. Indeed, we have seen fact patterns where the antirust crime is only part of the bad behavior engaged in by the leniency applicant.

While the department never has and never would use other criminal statutes to do an end-run around antitrust leniency, the point is that the leniency policy does not insulate corporations from all criminal exposure beyond the Sherman Act. Having said that, self-disclosure and cooperation are hallmarks of both the leniency policy and good corporate citizenship, and will be taken into account when the department considers criminal conduct outside the scope of the leniency application. The department assesses corporate charging decisions under the factors set forth in its Principles of Federal Prosecution of Business Organizations. Those factors place self-reporting, including of antitrust crimes, front-and-center in the charging calculus. So a leniency applicant, even if facing exposure for crimes outside the scope of the leniency policy, still benefits materially from reporting and cooperating with respect to both its antitrust and non-antitrust crimes.

The Division and the public benefit too. Experience teaches that our investigations often proceed more quickly with a cooperating leniency applicant. Early cooperation allows us to develop the facts quickly, in some cases by using covert techniques to expose more information about the nature and extent of the conspiracy.

In addition, the prospect that there may be a cooperating corporation in an antitrust investigation has changed the calculus for the other corporate co-conspirators. When an investigation becomes public, for example when we serve grand jury subpoenas or execute search warrants, price fixers face a real life prisoners' dilemma. They and their lawyers must consider whether there is a cooperating company—a leniency applicant. The rational fear that someone already is cooperating provides a strong motivation to conduct prompt internal investigations and early assessments of criminal exposure. If there is a problem, companies need to assume that the division probably already knows about it. As a result, we are seeing more companies approach the division at early stages of our cartel investigations, seeking to mitigate the consequences of their criminal wrongdoing.

We encourage that. It is the right thing to do. Even if a company is too late to qualify for leniency, we take early acceptance of responsibility and meaningful cooperation into account in determining the appropriate consequences for offending corporations and their executives.

It is important to keep separate these two concepts – acceptance of responsibility and cooperation that substantially assists the division. A company accepts responsibility when it truthfully acknowledges it has violated the law and agrees to plead guilty. Under the Sentencing Guidelines, companies that choose to accept responsibility will receive a lower culpability score, and therefore a lower fine range. Companies that delay owning up to their role in the antitrust conspiracy do not receive that consideration and the division will seek fines from progressively higher points in the fine range.

Cooperation requires more than accepting responsibility, though. Companies that approach us early and advance our investigations in meaningful ways will see that cooperation credited in our approach to their sentences. But, as with corporate leniency, promises to cooperate are not enough. Significant reductions in criminal sentences for substantial assistance will be reserved for those companies that actually help us investigate and prosecute antitrust crimes, as described in Chapter 8 of the Sentencing Guidelines.

A related point is that our sentencing recommendations will be based on the value of the cooperation we receive, not simply on the order in which companies begin to cooperate. Of course, companies that accept responsibility and begin cooperating sooner will have a greater chance to provide substantial assistance when it is most needed; the longer a company waits to cooperate, the less likely it is that the cooperation will have value to the division. That said, companies that begin cooperating later in the process still have a chance to mitigate the consequences of their wrongdoing – they can and often do provide substantial assistance by expanding the scope of our investigation or reporting an entirely new conspiracy. If a company that begins cooperating later provides substantial assistance, we will take that cooperation into account when making our sentencing recommendations.

When we negotiate corporate plea agreements we are also prepared to discuss the appropriate treatment of company executives and employees. We have said before and will continue to insist that the most culpable employees face the consequences of their crimes. They must accept responsibility and plead guilty or they will face indictment and trial. For other employees—those who seek protection through the non-prosecution agreements usually included in the division's corporate plea agreements—we expect full cooperation, and will revoke that protection for anyone who does not fully and truthfully cooperate with our investigations.

When we agree to include individuals in the non-prosecution provisions of a corporate plea agreement—so called "carve ins"—we need to specify those who are not entitled to that protection. We refer to those individuals as being excluded, or "carved out," of the corporate plea agreement. As many of you are aware, last year we decided to limit carve-outs from corporate plea agreements to those we have reason to believe were involved in criminal wrongdoing and who are potential targets of our investigation. To avoid publicly identifying those persons unless and until we charge them, we list their names in a confidential addendum to the corporate plea agreement, and ask the court to seal it.

Carve-out decisions will continue to be made on an employee-by-employee basis. Some have suggested that the number of carve-outs should be tied exclusively to the order in which companies come forward to accept responsibility and offer cooperation. That is not how we look at things. We apply the Principles of Federal Prosecution and consider such factors as the employee's role in the conspiracy, seniority in the company, and the assistance the employee is able to provide in bringing other wrongdoers to justice. Our decisions are based ultimately on these factors, not mechanically on the order in which the company chose to accept responsibility or chose to cooperate.

Obviously, the easiest way for companies and their executives to avoid prosecution is not to commit crimes. There has been a lot of important work done recently by the International Chamber of Commerce, the ABA, and others to encourage corporations to step up their compliance efforts. We think that is great. Effective compliance programs minimize the chance that companies will conspire to fix prices. And they maximize the chance for a company guilty of price fixing to find out about the conspiracy early enough to qualify for corporate leniency or otherwise cooperate with our investigation.

Some have argued that the mere existence of a compliance program should be sufficient, in and of itself, to avoid prosecution, secure a non-prosecution agreement, or otherwise dramatically reduce the penalties for criminal antitrust violations. That is something of a stretch. The fact that the company participated in a cartel, and did not detect it until after the investigation began, makes it difficult for the company to establish that its compliance program was effective. It is unlikely that a corporate defendant's pre-existing compliance and ethics program will be considered effective enough to warrant a slap on the wrist when it failed to prevent the company from violating the antitrust laws. This is a view we share with other parts of the department that prosecute corporate crimes.

We also expect companies to take compliance seriously once they have pleaded guilty or have been convicted. Taking compliance seriously includes making an institutional commitment to change the culture of the company. Companies should be fostering a corporate culture that encourages ethical conduct and a commitment to compliance with the law.

As Deputy Attorney General Cole has said, corporate compliance starts at the top. The board of directors and senior officers must set the tone for compliance to ensure that the company's entire managerial workforce not only understands the compliance program but also has the incentive to actively participate in its enforcement. Employees should be encouraged to report or seek guidance about potential criminal conduct without fear of retaliation, and there should be appropriate disciplinary measures for engaging in criminal conduct and for failing to take reasonable steps to prevent or detect that conduct.

Guilty companies sometimes want to continue to employ culpable senior executives who do not accept responsibility and are carved out of the corporate plea agreement, while at the same time arguing that their compliance programs are effective and their remediation efforts laudable. That creates an obvious tension. It is hard to imagine how companies can foster a corporate culture of compliance if they still employ individuals in positions with senior management and pricing responsibilities who have refused to accept responsibility for their crimes and who the companies know to be culpable. If any company continues to employ such individuals in positions of substantial authority; or in positions where they can continue to engage directly or indirectly in collusive conduct; or in positions where they supervise the company's compliance and remediation programs; or in positions where they supervise individuals who would be witnesses against them, we will have serious doubts about that company's commitment to implementing a new compliance program or invigorating an existing one. Indeed, the Sentencing Guidelines go so far as to suggest that companies that do so cannot be said to have an "effective" compliance program. In such cases, the division will consider seeking court-supervised probation as a means of assuring that the company devises and implements an effective compliance program. We reserve the right to insist on probation, including the use of monitors, if doing so is necessary to ensure an effective compliance program and to prevent recidivism.

The division recently faced a situation like this in our prosecution of AU Optronics. The jury found that AUO, its subsidiary, and its executives broke the law, and along with their conspirators, reaped an illicit gain of at least $500 million to the detriment of American consumers. While all of AUO's corporate co-conspirators recognized that their conspiracy was illegal and accepted responsibility for their participation in that scheme, AUO refused even to acknowledge that its participation in the same agreement was, or should be considered, illegal.

Far from demonstrating a commitment to future antitrust compliance, AUO continued to employ convicted price fixers and indicted fugitives. In those circumstances, the division argued that not only was probation necessary, but also a compliance monitor was appropriate. The district court agreed. It sentenced AUO and its U.S. subsidiary to three years of probation. The terms of probation required the companies to develop and implement an effective compliance and ethics program. And the companies were required to accept a compliance monitor whose job it is to supervise the implementation of the program and report back to the court and the division.

Convicted companies that implement effective compliance programs should not need to see us again. Companies that fail to do so, however, should expect significant penalties if we catch them again. For example, Bridgestone pleaded guilty several years ago for its role in the marine hose cartel. But at that time, Bridgestone did not disclose that it had also participated in a conspiracy to fix the price of anti-vibration rubber auto parts. Bridgestone's lackadaisical approach to compliance, demonstrated by its failure to disclose its participation in a second conspiracy, was treated as an aggravating factor in the calculation of its criminal fine when it pleaded guilty for its auto parts crimes. It was placed on probation and fined $425 million, the fourth-largest fine the division has ever obtained. The fine amount increased by over $100 million as a result of Bridgestone's failure to disclose the second conspiracy.

The bottom line is pretty simple. If a company commits an antitrust crime, it faces serious consequences here in the United States. A company can mitigate those consequences by coming forward promptly, cooperating completely, and taking the steps necessary to ensure that the conduct does not reoccur. The citizens of the United States are entitled to competitive markets free from collusion. We will work tirelessly to ensure that the benefits of competition continue to flow to the American consumer.

$1.4 billion

United Nations Security Council resolution 1158, adopted unanimously on 25 March 1998, after recalling all previous resolutions on Iraq, including resolutions 986 (1995), 1111 (1997), 1129 (1997), 1143 (1997) and 1153 (1998) concerning the Oil-for-Food Programme, the Council, acting under Chapter VII of the United Nations Charter, authorised the sale of up to 1.4 billion United States dollars of Iraqi oil and oil products within a 90-day period, beginning from 5 March 1998. The Security Council was concerned about the humanitarian consequences for the Iraqi people after the shortfall in the revenue from the sale of petroleum and petroleum products during the first 90-day period of implementation of Resolution 1143, due to a fall in oil prices and delayed resumption of oil sales by Iraq. It was determined to avoid the further deterioration of the humanitarian situation. Acting under Chapter VII, the Council decided that the mechanism whereby Iraqi oil exports, would finance humanitarian aid for a further 90 days, beginning at 00:01 EST on 5 March 1998. The sum of the sales could not exceed US$1.4 billion in the 90 day period.

25

25 (twenty-five) is the natural number following 24 and preceding 26.

$425 million

Hub Power Company Limited (HUBCO) is located at Hub, Lasbela District, Balochistan, Pakistan. The Hub Power Company is a large, private-sector power company and its 1,200 MW plant is located 60 km from Karachi in Hub. The electricity at HUBCO is generated by four 323 megawatt oil-fired units that are supplied by a 78 km long pipeline from Pakistan State Oil (HUBCO, 1999b). The oil is burned in 4 large boilers to produce steam to generate electricity. HUBCO received a loan agreement of US$ 425 million from the Government of Pakistan via the National Development Finance Corporation in 1994. It is considered one of the most successful private-public partnership projects in Pakistan. In 1996, a multi-effect distillation plant, manufactured by Sasakura-Japan, was commissioned, with a capacity of 3,600 cubic meters of water per day.

$500 million

NGC 1907 is an open star cluster around 4,500 light years from Earth. It contains around 30 stars and is over 500 million years old. With a magnitude of 8.2 it is visible as part of the constellation Auriga.

Antitrust Division

The United States Department of Justice Antitrust Division is responsible for enforcing the antitrust laws of the United States. It shares jurisdiction over civil antitrust cases with the Federal Trade Commission (FTC) and often works jointly with the FTC to provide regulatory guidance to businesses. However, the Antitrust Division also has the power to file criminal cases against willful violators of the antitrust laws. The Antitrust Division also works with competition regulators in other countries.

antitrust law

Competition law is a law that promotes or seeks to maintain market competition by regulating anti-competitive conduct by companies. Competition law is implemented through public and private enforcement. Competition law is known as antitrust law in the United States and anti-monopoly law in China and Russia. In previous years it has been known as trade practices law in the United Kingdom and Australia. The history of competition law reaches back to the Roman Empire. The business practices of market traders, guilds and governments have always been subject to scrutiny, and sometimes severe sanctions. Since the 20th century, competition law has become global. The two largest and most influential systems of competition regulation are United States antitrust law and European Union competition law. National and regional competition authorities across the world have formed international support and enforcement networks. Modern competition law has historically evolved on a country level to promote and maintain fair competition in markets principally within the territorial boundaries of nation-states. National competition law usually does not cover activity beyond territorial borders unless it has significant effects at nation-state level. Countries may allow for extraterritorial jurisdiction in competition cases based on so-called effects doctrine. The protection of international competition is governed by international competition agreements. In 1945, during the negotiations preceding the adoption of the General Agreement on Tariffs and Trade (GATT) in 1947, limited international competition obligations were proposed within the Charter for an International Trade Organisation. These obligations were not included in GATT, but in 1994, with the conclusion of the Uruguay Round of GATT Multilateral Negotiations, the World Trade Organization (WTO) was created. The Agreement Establishing the WTO included a range of limited provisions on various cross-border competition issues on a sector specific basis.

AU Optronics

AU Optronics (AUO) is a Taiwanese manufacturer of TFT LCD and other technologies that was formed in December 2001 by the merger of Acer Display Technology (established in 1996) and Unipac Optoelectronics Corporation by BenQ Electronics. In April 2006, AUO announced the purchase of Quanta Display, Inc. At the time of merger, the combined companies represented 17% of the global TFT-LCD market. The production of the company's G6 operation reached #1 worldwide. AUO manufactures TFT panels for companies including Samsung, Sony, NEC, Lenovo, Panasonic, LG, Dell, Apple, Viewsonic, Acer, Toshiba..

Bridgestone

The Bridgestone Corporation (, Kabushiki-gaisha Burijisuton) (TYO: 5108, OTC Pink: BRDCY) is a multinational auto and truck parts manufacturer founded in 1931 by Shojiro Ishibashi (, Ishibashi Shōjirō) in the city of Kurume, Fukuoka, Japan. The name Bridgestone comes from a calque translation and transposition of ishibashi, meaning "stone bridge" in Japanese. Production facilities belonging to the Bridgestone Group number 141 in twenty-four countries, as of the end of 2005.

California

California (/ kæl f rnjə/) is a state located on the West Coast of the United States. It is the most populous U.S. state, home to one out of eight people who live in the U.S., with a total of 38 million people, and it is the third largest state by area (after Alaska and Texas). California is bordered by Oregon to the north, Nevada to the east, Arizona to the southeast, and the Mexican state of Baja California to the south. It is home to the nation's second and fifth most populous census statistical areas (Greater Los Angeles Area and San Francisco Bay Area, respectively), and eight of the nation's 50 most populated cities (Los Angeles, San Diego, San Jose, San Francisco, Fresno, Sacramento, Long Beach, and Oakland). Sacramento is the state capital, and has been since 1854. What is now California was first settled by various Native American tribes before being explored by a number of European expeditions throughout the 16th and 17th centuries. It was then claimed by the Spanish Empire as part of Alta California in the larger territory of New Spain. Alta California became a part of Mexico in 1821 following its successful war for independence, but would later be ceded to the United States in 1848 after the Mexican-American War. The western portion of Alta California was soon organized as the State of California, which was admitted as the 31st state on September 9, 1850. The California

Gold Rush starting in 1848 led to dramatic social and demographic change, with large-scale immigration from the east and abroad with an accompanying economic boom. California's diverse geography ranges from the Pacific Coast in the west, to the Sierra Nevada in the east – from the Redwood–Douglas fir forests of the northwest, to the Mojave Desert areas in the southeast. The center of the state is dominated by the Central Valley, a major agricultural area. California contains both the highest and lowest points in the contiguous United States (Mount Whitney and Death Valley), and has the 3rd longest coastline of all states (after Alaska and Florida). Earthquakes are a common occurrence because of the state's location along the Pacific Ring of Fire: about 37,000 are recorded annually, but most are too small to feel. At least half of the fruit produced in the United States is now cultivated in California, and the state also leads in the production of vegetables. Other important contributors to the state's economy include aerospace, education, manufacturing, and high-tech industry. If it were a country, California would be the 8th or 9th largest economy in the world and the 34th most populous.

Chamber of Commerce

A chamber of commerce (or board of trade) is a form of business network, e.g., a local organization of businesses whose goal is to further the interests of businesses. Business owners in towns and cities form these local societies to advocate on behalf of the business community. Local businesses are members, and they elect a board of directors or executive council to set policy for the chamber. The board or council then hires a President, CEO or Executive Director, plus staffing appropriate to size, to run the organization. The first chamber of commerce was founded in 1599 in Marseille, France. It would be followed 65 years later by another official chamber of commerce, probably in Bruges, then part of the Spanish Netherlands. The world's oldest English-speaking chamber of commerce is that of New York City, which was established in 1768. The oldest known existing chamber in the English-speaking world with continuous records is the Glasgow Chamber of Commerce, which was founded in 1783. However, Hull Chamber of Commerce is the UK's oldest, followed by Leeds and Belfast, Northern Ireland. A chamber of commerce is not a governmental body or institution, and has no direct role in the writing and passage of laws and regulations that affect businesses. It may however, act as a lobby in an attempt to get laws passed that are favorable to businesses.

Congress

A congress is a formal meeting of the representatives of different nations, constituent states, independent organizations (such as trade unions), or groups. The term was chosen for the Continental Congress to emphasize the status of each colony represented there as a self-governing unit. Subsequent to the use of congress by the U.S. legislature, the term has been adopted by many states within unions, and by unitary nation-states in the Americas, to refer to their legislatures.

Dean Treanor

Dean Leroy Treanor (born December 8, 1947) is an American professional baseball manager. Since 2011, he has been the field boss of the Indianapolis Indians, Triple-A farm system affiliate of the Pittsburgh Pirates in the International League. He is a native and resident of San Luis Obispo, California. Treanor was a right-handed pitcher during his playing days who stood 5 feet 10 inches (1.78 m) tall and weighed 150 pounds (68 kg). He attended Cal Poly San Luis Obispo. There is some discrepancy among sources regarding Treanor's professional playing career. The Indians' official website states that he signed with the Cincinnati Reds and progressed as high as the Double-A level with the Trois-Rivières Aigles of the Eastern League. However, his page on Baseball Reference lists only two total pitching appearances with the Fresno Suns in 1988 (at age 40) and Reno Silver Sox in 1991 (at 43), both of the Class A California League. In 2011, MLB.com reported that Treanor's playing career was cut short by a rotator cuff injury in 1975, and that he spent 13 years as a police officer and undercover narcotics agent in his hometown. In 1988, Treanor returned to baseball as a minor league manager and pitching coach, working in the organizations of the Cleveland Indians, San Diego Padres, Montreal Expos, Los Angeles Dodgers and Florida Marlins. He has managed at the highest level of the minor leagues from 2002–2003, 2005–2008, and since 2011 in the Marlins' and Pirates' organizations with the Calgary Cannons, Albuquerque Isotopes, and Indianapolis. He also served as a pitching coach with the Double-A Altoona Curve (2009) and Triple-A Indianapolis (2010). According to the Indianapolis Indians' official website, Treanor is only the eighth Indians' manager in the Indians' 113-year history to have helmed the club for four or more consecutive seasons. He won back-to-back division championships in 2012–2013. His 11-season career record as a skipper is 799–771 (.509).

EPA

The United States Environmental Protection Agency (EPA or sometimes USEPA) is an agency of the U.S. federal government which was created for the purpose of protecting human health and the environment by writing and enforcing regulations based on laws passed by Congress. The EPA was proposed by President Richard Nixon and began operation on December 2, 1970, after Nixon signed an executive order. The order establishing the EPA was ratified by committee hearings in the House and Senate. The agency is led by its Administrator, who is appointed by the president and approved by Congress. The current administrator is Gina McCarthy. The EPA is not a Cabinet department, but the administrator is normally given cabinet rank. The EPA has its headquarters in Washington, D.C., regional offices for each of the agency's ten regions, and 27 laboratories. The agency conducts environmental assessment, research, and education. It has the responsibility of maintaining and enforcing national standards under a variety of environmental laws, in consultation with state, tribal, and local governments. It delegates some permitting, monitoring, and enforcement responsibility to U.S. states and the federally recognized tribes. EPA enforcement powers include fines, sanctions, and other measures. The agency also works with industries and all levels of government in a wide variety of voluntary pollution prevention programs and energy conservation efforts. The agency has approximately 15,193 full-time employees and engages many more people on a contractual basis. More than half of EPA human resources are engineers, scientists, and environmental protection specialists; other groups include legal, public affairs, financial, and information technologists.

FBI

The Federal Bureau of Investigation (FBI) is a governmental agency belonging to the United States Department of Justice that serves as both a federal criminal investigative organization and an internal intelligence agency. The FBI is the lead U.S. counterterrorism agency and the lead U.S. counterintelligence agency. It is the USA's security service, and is a component agency of the U.S. Intelligence Community. Also, it is the government agency responsible for investigating crimes on sovereign Native American reservations in the United States under the Major Crimes Act. The FBI has investigative jurisdiction over violations of more than 200 categories of federal crime. The bureau was established in 1908 as the Bureau of Investigation (BOI). Its name was changed to the Federal Bureau of Investigation (FBI) in 1935. The FBI headquarters is the J. Edgar Hoover Building, located in Washington, D.C. The bureau has fifty-six field offices located in major cities throughout the United States, and more than 400 resident agencies in lesser cities and areas across the nation. More than 50 international offices called "legal attachés" exist in U.S. embassies and consulates general worldwide.

fraud

Fraud is a deception deliberately practiced in order to secure unfair or unlawful gain (adjectival form fraudulent; to defraud is the verb). As a legal construct, fraud is both a civil wrong (i.e., a fraud victim may sue the fraud perpetrator to avoid the fraud and/or recover monetary compensation) and a criminal wrong (i.e., a fraud perpetrator may be prosecuted and imprisoned by governmental authorities). Defrauding people or organizations of money or valuables is the usual purpose of fraud, but it sometimes instead involves obtaining benefits without actually depriving anyone of money or valuables, such as obtaining a drivers license by way of false statements made in an application for the same. A hoax is a distinct concept that involves deception without the intention of gain or of materially damaging or depriving the victim.

free market

A free market is a market system in which the prices for goods and services are set freely by consent between sellers and consumers, in which the laws and forces of supply and demand are free from any intervention by a government, price-setting monopoly, or other authority. A free market contrasts with a controlled market or regulated market, in which government intervenes in supply and demand through non-market methods such as laws creating barriers to market entry or directly setting prices. A free market economy is a market-based economy where prices for goods and services are set freely by the forces of supply and demand and are allowed to reach their point of equilibrium without intervention by government policy, and it typically entails support for highly competitive markets and private ownership of productive enterprises. Although free markets are commonly associated with capitalism in contemporary usage and popular culture, free markets have been advocated by market anarchists, market socialists, and some proponents of cooperatives and advocates of profit sharing.

Georgetown University Law Center

Georgetown University Law Center (also known as Georgetown Law) is the law school of Georgetown University, located in Washington, D.C. Established in 1870, the Law Center offers J.D., LL.M., and S.J.D. degrees in law. As the second largest law school in the United States, Georgetown Law often touts the advantages of its wide range of program offerings and proximity to federal agencies and courts, including the Supreme Court. The Law Center is one of the 14 law schools that consistently place at the top of U.S. News & World Report's annual rankings.

million

One million (1,000,000) or one thousand thousand, is the natural number following 999,999 and preceding 1,000,001. The word is derived from the early

Italian millione (milione in modern Italian), from mille, "thousand", plus the augmentative suffix -one. In scientific notation, it is written as 1×10^6 or just 10^6. Physical quantities can also be expressed using the SI prefix mega, when dealing with SI units. For example, 1 megawatt equals 1,000,000 watts. It can be abbreviated MM, mm or mn in some financial contexts. The meaning of the word "million" is common to the short scale and long scale numbering systems, unlike the larger numbers, which have different names in the two systems. The million is sometimes used in the English language as a metaphor for a very large number, as in "Never in a million years" and "You're one in a million", or a hyperbole, as in "I've walked a million miles" and "You've asked the million-dollar question".

months

A month is a unit of time, used with calendars, which is approximately as long as a natural period related to the motion of the Moon; month and Moon are cognates. The traditional concept arose with the cycle of moon phases; such months (lunations) are synodic months and last approximately 29.53 days. From excavated tally sticks, researchers have deduced that people counted days in relation to the Moon's phases as early as the Paleolithic age. Synodic months, based on the Moon's orbital period with respect to the Earth-Sun line, are still the basis of many calendars today, and are used to divide the year.

New Jersey

New Jersey is a state in the Northeastern and Middle Atlantic regions of the United States. It is bordered on the north and east by New York State, on the southeast and south by the Atlantic Ocean, on the west by Pennsylvania, and on the southwest by Delaware. New Jersey is the fourth-smallest state, but the 11th-most populous and the most densely populated of the 50 United States. New Jersey lies entirely within the combined statistical areas of New York City and Philadelphia. It is also the second-wealthiest U.S. state by median household income, according to the 2008–2012 American Community Survey. The area was inhabited by Native Americans for more than 2,800 years, with historical tribes such as the Lenape along the coast. In the early 17th century, the Dutch and the Swedes made the first European settlements. The English later seized control of the region, naming it the Province of New Jersey. It was granted as a colony to Sir George Carteret and John Berkeley, 1st Baron Berkeley of Stratton. At this time, it was named after the largest of the Channel Islands, Jersey, Carteret's birthplace. New Jersey was the site of several decisive battles during the American Revolutionary War. In the 19th century, factories in cities such as Camden, Paterson, Newark, Trenton, and Elizabeth helped to drive the Industrial Revolution. New Jersey's geographic location at the center of the Northeast megalopolis, between Boston and New York City to the northeast, and Philadelphia, Baltimore, and Washington, D.C., to the southwest, fueled its rapid growth through the process of suburbanization in the 1950s and beyond.

Ninth Circuit

The United States Court of Appeals for the Ninth Circuit (in case citations, 9th Cir.) is a U.S. Federal court with appellate jurisdiction over the district courts in the following districts: District of Alaska District of Arizona Central District of California Eastern District of California Northern District of California Southern District of California District of Hawaii District of Idaho District of Montana District of Nevada District of Oregon Eastern District of Washington Western District of Washington It also has appellate jurisdiction over the following territorial courts: District of Guam District of the Northern Mariana Islands Headquartered in San Francisco, California, the Ninth Circuit is by far the largest of the thirteen courts of appeals, with 29 active judgeships. The court's regular meeting places are Seattle at the William K. Nakamura Courthouse, Portland at the Pioneer Courthouse, San Francisco at the James R. Browning U.S. Court of Appeals Building, and Pasadena at the Richard H. Chambers U.S. Court of Appeals. Panels of the court occasionally travel to hear cases in other locations within the circuit. Although the judges travel around the circuit, the court arranges its hearings so that cases from the northern region of the circuit are heard in Seattle or Portland, cases from southern California are heard in Pasadena, and cases from northern California, Nevada, Arizona, and Hawaii are heard in San Francisco. For lawyers who must come and present their cases to the court in person, this administrative grouping of cases helps to reduce the time and cost of travel.

price fixing

Price fixing is an agreement between participants on the same side in a market to buy or sell a product, service, or commodity only at a fixed price, or maintain the market conditions such that the price is maintained at a given level by controlling supply and demand. The intent of price fixing may be to push the price of a product as high as possible, generally leading to profits for all sellers but may also have the goal to fix, peg, discount, or stabilize prices. The defining characteristic of price fixing is any agreement regarding price, whether expressed or implied. Price fixing requires a conspiracy between sellers or buyers. The purpose is to coordinate pricing for mutual benefit of the traders. For example, manufacturers and retailers may conspire to sell at a common "retail" price; set a common minimum sales price, where sellers agree not to discount the sales price below the agreed-to minimum price; buy the product from a supplier at a specified maximum price; adhere to a price book or list price; engage in cooperative price advertising; standardize financial credit terms offered to purchasers; use uniform trade-in allowances; limit discounts; discontinue a free service or fix the price of one component of an overall service; adhere uniformly to previously-announced prices and terms of sale; establish uniform costs and markups; impose mandatory surcharges; purposefully reduce output or sales in order to charge higher prices; or purposefully share or pool markets, territories, or customers. Price fixing is permitted in some markets but not others; where allowed, it is often known as resale price maintenance or retail price maintenance. In neo-classical economics, price fixing is inefficient. The anti-competitive agreement by producers to fix prices above the market price transfers some of the consumer surplus to those producers and also results in a deadweight loss. International price fixing by private entities can be prosecuted under the antitrust laws of many countries. Examples of prosecuted international cartels are those that controlled the prices and output of lysine, citric acid, graphite electrodes, and bulk vitamins.

project manager

A project manager is a professional in the field of project management. Project managers can have the responsibility of the planning, execution and closing of any project, typically relating to construction industry, architecture, aerospace and defense, computer networking, telecommunications or software development. Many other fields in the production, design and service industries also have project managers.

real estate market

Real estate is "property consisting of land and the buildings on it, along with its natural resources such as crops, minerals, or water; immovable property of this nature; an interest vested in this; (also) an item of real property; (more generally) buildings or housing in general. Also: the business of real estate; the profession of buying, selling, or renting land, buildings or housing." It is a legal term used in jurisdictions such as the United States, United Kingdom, Canada, Nigeria, Australia, and New Zealand.

search warrants

A search warrant is a court order issued by a magistrate, judge or Supreme Court official that authorizes law enforcement officers to conduct a search of a person, location, or vehicle for evidence of a crime and to confiscate evidence if it is found. A search warrant cannot be issued in aid of civil process. Jurisdictions that respect the rule of law and a right to privacy put constraints on the powers of police investigators, and typically require search warrants, or an equivalent procedure, for searches conducted as part of a criminal investigation. An exception is usually made for hot pursuit: if a criminal flees the scene of a crime and the police officer follows him, the officer has the right to enter a property in which the criminal has sought shelter. Conversely, in authoritarian regimes, the police typically have the right to search property and people without having to provide justification, or without having to secure the permission of a court.

Senate

A senate is a deliberative assembly, often the upper house or chamber of a bicameral legislature or parliament. The name comes from the ancient Roman Senate, so-called as an assembly of the senior and thus wiser members of the society or ruling class. Many countries currently have an assembly named a senate, composed of senators who may be elected, appointed, have inherited the title, or gained membership by other methods, depending on the country. Modern senates typically serve to provide a chamber of "sober second thought" to consider legislation passed by a lower house, whose members are usually elected.

Sherman Act

The Sherman Antitrust Act (Sherman Act,26 Stat. 209, 15 U.S.C. §§ 1–7) is a landmark federal statute in the history of United States antitrust law (or "competition law") passed by Congress in 1890. It prohibits certain business activities that federal government regulators deem to be anti-competitive, and requires the federal government to investigate and pursue trusts. It has since, more broadly, been used to oppose the combination of entities that could potentially harm competition, such as monopolies or cartels. According to its authors, it was not intended to impact market gains obtained by honest means, by benefiting the consumers more than the competitors. Senator George Hoar of Massachusetts, another author of the Sherman act, said the following:

"... [a person] who merely by superior skill and intelligence...got the whole business because nobody could do it as well as he could was not a monopolist..(but was if) it involved something like the use of means which made it impossible for other persons to engage in fair competition."

Its reference to trusts today is anachronistic. At the time of its passage, the trust was synonymous with monopolistic practice, because the trust was a popular way for monopolists to hold their businesses, and a way for cartel participants to create enforceable agreements. In 1879, C. T. Dodd, an attorney for the Standard Oil Company of Ohio, devised a new type of trust agreement to overcome prohibitions in Ohio against corporations owning stock in other corporations. A trust is an otherwise neutral, centuries-old form of a contract whereby one party entrusts its property to a second party. The property is then used to benefit the first party. The law attempts to prevent the artificial raising of prices by restriction of trade or supply. In other words, innocent monopoly, or monopoly achieved solely by merit, is perfectly legal, but acts by a monopolist to artificially preserve his status, or nefarious dealings to create a monopoly, are not. Put another way, it has sometimes been said that the purpose of the Sherman Act is not to protect competitors, but rather to protect competition, as well as promote and preserve a competitive landscape. As explained by the U.S. Supreme Court in Spectrum Sports, Inc. v. McQuillan 506 U.S. 447 (1993):

The purpose of the [Sherman] Act is not to protect businesses from the working of the market; it is to protect the public from the failure of the market. The law directs itself not against conduct which is competitive, even severely so, but against conduct which unfairly tends to destroy competition itself.

"This focus of U.S. competition law, on protection of competition rather than competitors, is not necessarily the only possible focus or purpose of competition law. For example, it has also been said that competition law in the European Union (EU) tends to protect the competitors in the marketplace, even at the expense of market efficiencies and consumers."

tax evasion

Tax evasion is the illegal evasion of taxes by individuals, corporations and trusts. Tax evasion often entails taxpayers deliberately misrepresenting the true state of their affairs to the tax authorities to reduce their tax liability and includes dishonest tax reporting, such as declaring less income, profits or gains than the amounts actually earned, or overstating deductions. Tax evasion is an activity commonly associated with the informal economy. One measure of the extent of tax evasion (the "tax gap") is the amount of unreported income, which is the difference between the amount of income that should be reported to the tax authorities and the actual amount reported. In contrast, tax avoidance is the legal use of tax laws to reduce one's tax burden. Both tax evasion and avoidance can be viewed as forms of tax noncompliance, as they describe a range of activities that intend to subvert a state's tax system, although such classification of tax avoidance is not indisputable, given that avoidance is lawful, within self-creating systems.

United States

The United States of America (USA or U.S.A.), commonly referred to as the United States (US or U.S.), America, and sometimes the States, is a federal republic consisting of 50 states and a federal district. The 48 contiguous states and Washington, D.C., are in central North America between Canada and Mexico. The state of Alaska is the northwestern part of North America and the state of Hawaii is an archipelago in the mid-Pacific. The country also has five populated and nine unpopulated territories in the Pacific and the Caribbean. At 3.80 million square miles (9.85 million km2) and with around 318 million people, the United States is the world's third- or fourth-largest country by total area and third-largest by population. It is one of the world's most ethnically diverse and multicultural nations, the product of large-scale immigration from many countries. The geography and climate of the United States is also extremely diverse, and it is home to a wide variety of wildlife. Paleo-Indians migrated from Eurasia to what is now the U.S. mainland around 15,000 years ago, with European colonization beginning in the 16th century. The United States emerged from 13 British colonies located along the Atlantic seaboard. Disputes between Great Britain and these colonies led to the American Revolution. On July 4, 1776, as the colonies were fighting Great Britain in the American Revolutionary War, delegates from the 13 colonies unanimously issued the Declaration of Independence. The war ended in 1783 with the recognition of independence of the United States from the Kingdom of Great Britain, and was the first successful war of independence against a European colonial empire. The current Constitution was adopted on September 17, 1787. The first ten amendments, collectively named the Bill of Rights, were ratified in 1791 and designed to guarantee many fundamental civil rights and freedoms. Driven by the doctrine of manifest destiny, the United States embarked on a vigorous expansion across North America throughout the 19th century. This involved displacing native tribes, acquiring new territories, and gradually admitting new states. During the second half of the 19th century, the American Civil War ended legal slavery in the country. By the end of that century, the United States extended into the Pacific Ocean, and its economy began to soar. The Spanish–American War and World War I confirmed the country's status as a global military power. The United States emerged from World War II as a global superpower, the first country to develop nuclear weapons, the only country to use them in warfare, and as a permanent member of the United Nations Security Council. The end of the Cold War and the dissolution of the Soviet Union left the United States as the sole superpower. The United States is a developed country and has the world's largest national economy. The economy is fueled by an abundance of natural resources and high worker productivity. While the U.S. economy is considered post-industrial, it continues to be one of the world's largest manufacturers. The country accounts for 37% of global military spending, being the world's foremost economic and military power, a prominent political and cultural force, and a leader in scientific research and technological innovations.

www.ingramcontent.com/pod-product-compliance
Lightning Source LLC
Chambersburg PA
CBHW081812170526
45167CB00008B/3416